Ribbon
Embroidery

Natalie Bellanger-Clément

Ribbon Embroidery

Simple Stitches for Easy Embellishments

Photographs by Francis Waldman
Design by Sonia Lucano
Written by Dominique Montembault

POTTER
CRAFT

New York

Wide and narrow, floating and sheer, plain and multicolored, matte and shimmering—ribbon comes in a seemingly infinite and ever-changing range. Embroidering with ribbon uses so many combinations of colors and materials that a play of textures and tones—combinations that allow you to express your creativity—makes this form of embroidery quite fascinating. You only need the basic items used in all embroidery—pins, embroidery hoop, embroidery scissors—plus DMC chenille needles with large eyes and some pinking shears to give your work a neat finish.

Embroidering with ribbon is a simple process with unfailingly spectacular results. In a matter of moments a translucent dragonfly can alight on the fabric, a pattern of delicate roses can grow from a background of seed stitches, or leaves and ferns can entwine on a featherstitch border. Organza hovers over the fabric, silk rubs shoulders with linen; soft, romantic touches are everywhere.

Ribbon can also be used in conjunction with embroidery thread; try combining lines of stitches or weave them together in a mixture of colors and textures. As if by magic, one stitch leads to another, patterns crisscross, and what starts as a pastime rapidly turns into a passion.

Ribbon embroidery is truly a never-ending fascination.

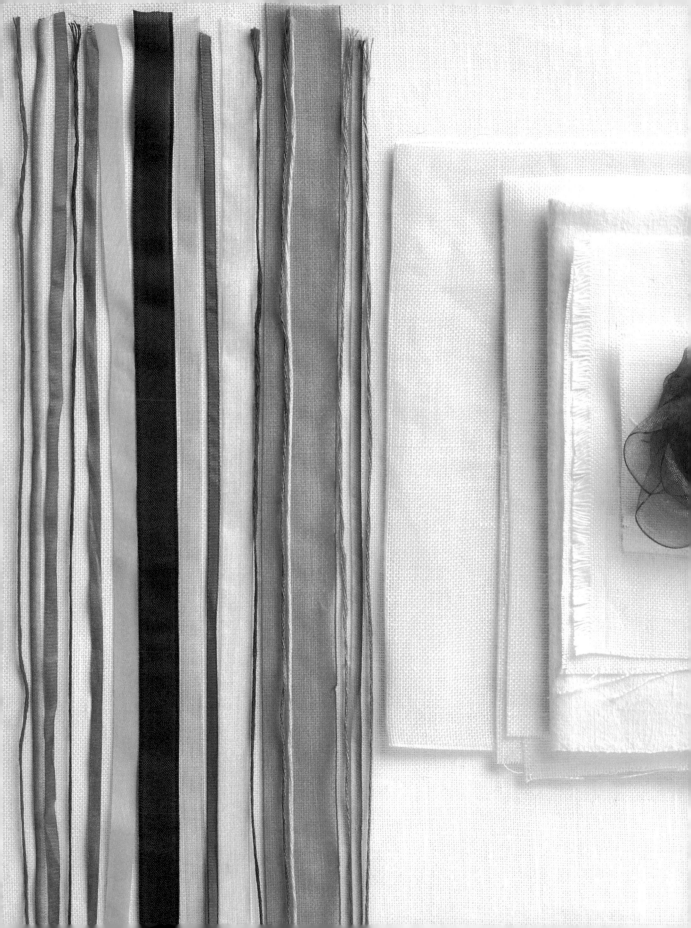

Table of Contents

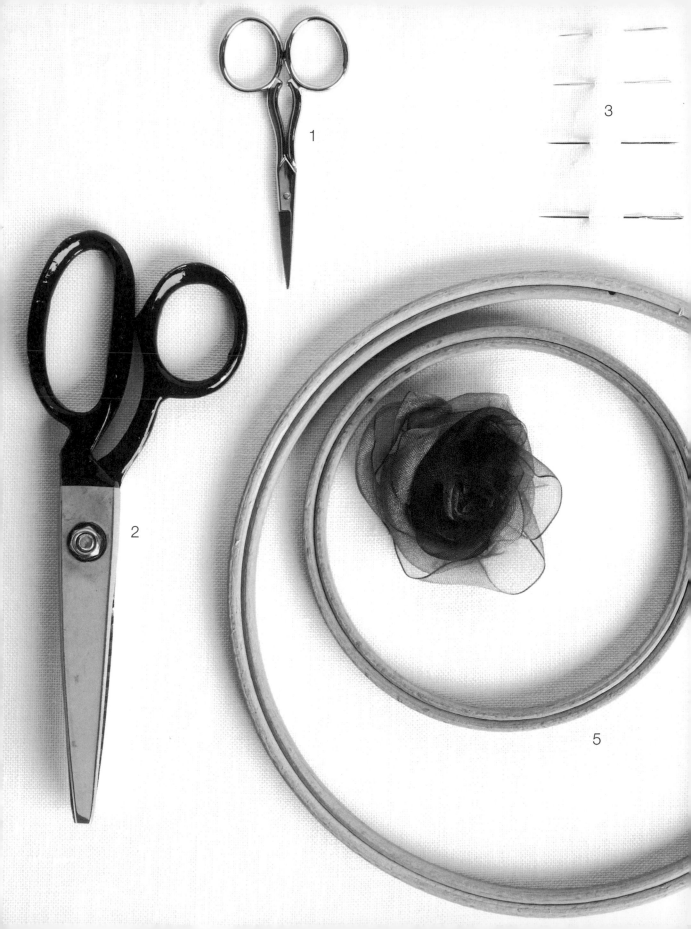

4

Tools and Materials

Tools

1   Embroidery scissors

2   Pinking shears

3   Chenille needles

4   Straight pins

5   embroidery hoops

Materials

(see page 6, from left to right)

Assorted ribbons

6-strand embroidery floss

White linen embroidery fabric,
30 threads/inch (12 threads/cm)

Tips and Techniques

Ribbon is actually an easy material to use for embroidery. However, a few practical hints will be useful if you are a beginner and it's a good idea to read these pages carefully before starting out. These little techniques will save time and make the stitches easier to recreate.

To reproduce a template

Ribbon embroidery loses its texture if it is washed, so it is better not to draw or trace the motifs. Outlining the contours of the design with pins should generally give an adequate guide to follow.

Photocopy your motif to the size required. Use dressmaker's carbon paper, which is made specifically for use with fabric.

Place the carbon paper between the motif and the fabric and trace the contour very lightly with a pencil (0.7 mm).

To thread a needle with narrow ribbon

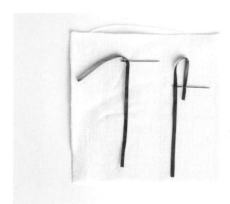

Slip the ribbon through the eye of the needle, making sure that it stays flat, then slide the needle a few inches down the ribbon. Make a loop in the ribbon and insert the point of the needle into the ribbon about ⅜ inch from the end.

Hold the needle in one hand and pull lightly with the other on the longer end of ribbon until it comes close to the needle's eye, a little like a running knot. This locks the ribbon onto the needle and allows you to work without the ribbon slipping off the needle.

To thread a needle with wide ribbon

When using wide ribbon, you may have difficulty threading it through the eye of the needle. To make it easier, fold the ribbon width carefully in two, three, or even four (making sure that it doesn't crumple), and push it gently through the eye.

 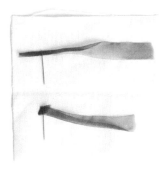

Working with sheer ribbon

Start by ironing the ribbon you intend to use with a warm iron. This will make it smoother and easier to handle.

Finishing ribbon with a knot

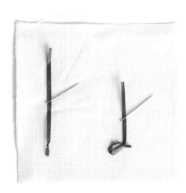

Tie a knot at one end of the ribbon, just as you would in a length of embroidery thread. Then insert the needle into the ribbon between the knot and the end.

Finishing ribbon without a knot

Knots should never be used where they will be unsightly, especially on fine fabric. Luckily, there are several ways to avoid making a knot at the start of the work that will ensure the reverse side is neat and tidy. The correct finishing is equally important. Never forget that the quality of embroidery is judged by the way it looks on both the front and the back of the fabric.

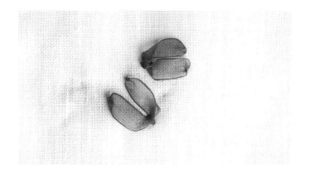

Stitches made in feather-light ribbon on fine fabric must be impeccably finished on the reverse side or there is a risk of the ends showing through.

To secure the end of the ribbon, tuck it under the back of a few stitches, then anchor it with a stitch or two of sewing thread.

To start without knotting the ribbon, leave 1–1½" at the back of the work and temporarily secure with a pin. When the embroidery is finished, anchor the ribbon with a few stitches of sewing thread and cut away the excess.

Finishing embroidery thread without a knot

When creating a framework using embroidery thread through which ribbon is to be woven, it is better not to leave a knot of cotton on the reverse side. Double a length of embroidery thread and pass both ends through the needle eye. Bring the needle up through the work, leaving a loop at the back, then insert the needle just to the side to form a small stitch. Pass the needle through the loop of thread and pull tight.

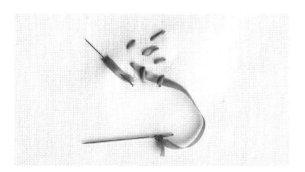

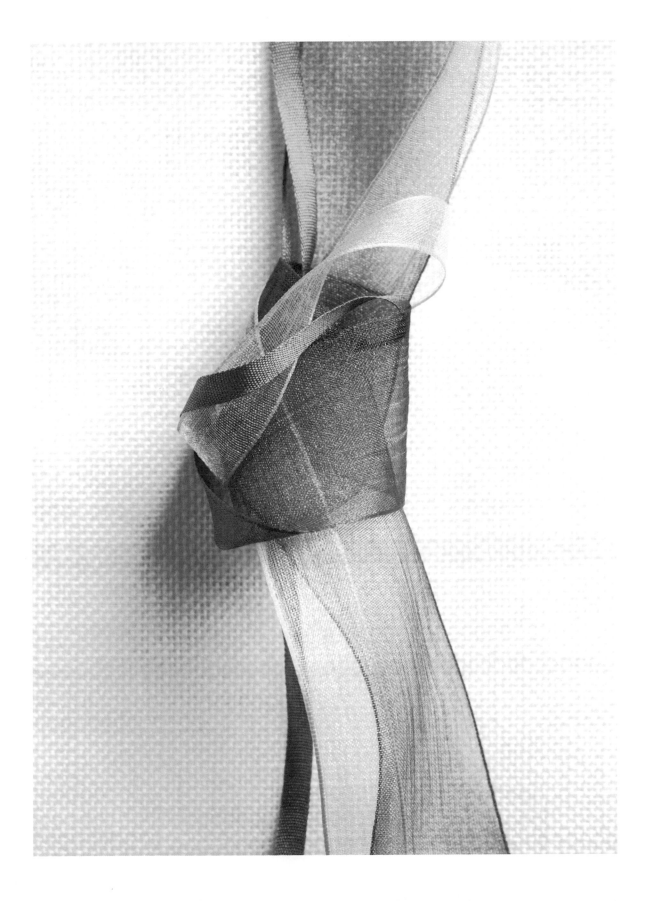

Small repeating stitches

Like seeds blown by the wind, these stitches are fanciful little touches that give fabric a cheerful sparkle. Light and delicate, a sprinkling of small motifs can form the perfect background to more complex designs. To make the sampler illustrated opposite, see the instructions on page 28.

Fly stitch template page 57

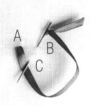

1. Bring the ribbon through at A, insert the needle at B, and bring out at C, keeping the ribbon flat.

2. Insert again at D, on the other side of the ribbon in order to pin the fly stitch firmly to the fabric.

3. This simple stitch can be repeated over and over in different sizes, using ribbon of all kinds.

Note With sheer ribbon the result will be light and airy.

Variation Two superimposed stitches in different color ribbons give a raised effect.

Variation It is also possible to mix textures and colors to give contrasting results.

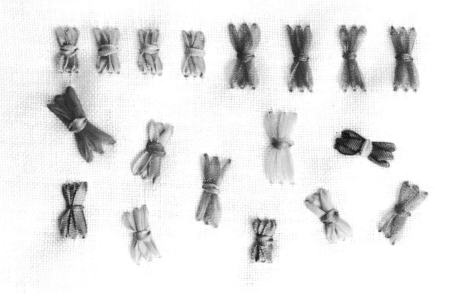

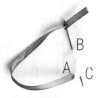

1. Bring the needle out at A, insert it higher up at B, and bring out the point at C.

2. Form a second straight stitch in the same way, very close to the first stitch.

3. Form a third stitch by pulling the needle through to the back of the fabric.

 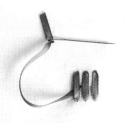

4. Push the needle through to the front of the fabric under the center of the second stitch at D.

5. Slide the needle under the first stitch, bringing the ribbon out to the left of the first stitch.

6. Pass the ribbon over all three stitches. Reinsert the needle at D, pulling the ribbon tight at the back.

Lazy daisy stitch template page 57

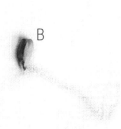

1. Bring the needle out at A, reinsert it at the same point, and pull it through the fabric.

2. Pull on the ribbon to form a small loop and bring the needle out at B, passing it through the loop.

3. Insert the needle at C and pull it through the fabric.

4. Pull the ribbon tight so that the loop is secured to the fabric.

Variation Create a motif from several single loops in different colors.

Variation You can also make loops of one color framed in other loops of a different color.

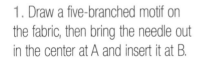

1. Draw a five-branched motif on the fabric, then bring the needle out in the center at A and insert it at B.

2. Pull the ribbon through so that it lies quite flat, then bring the needle out at C and insert at D.

3. Flatten the ribbon firmly against the fabric, then bring the needle out at E and insert at F.

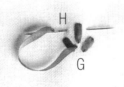

4. Flatten the ribbon firmly against the fabric, then bring the needle out at G and insert at H.

5. Make a final stitch on the fifth branch, then anchor the ribbon on the back of the fabric.

Variation With a different ribbon, make smaller straight stitches starting at the base of each of the large ones.

Woven wheel template page 57

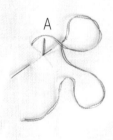 

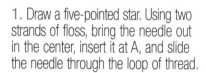

1. Draw a five-pointed star. Using two strands of floss, bring the needle out in the center, insert it at A, and slide the needle through the loop of thread.

2. Form all the points of the star using straight stitches (page 24) and finish off the thread on the reverse side of the fabric.

3. Using ribbon, bring the needle out in the center of the star between two straight stitches.

4. Pass the needle and the ribbon under the left-hand stitch and over the next one.

5. Pull the ribbon tight and pass the needle over then under for the next two stitches.

6. Continue to weave the ribbon in and out of the stitches until the wheel is completely full.

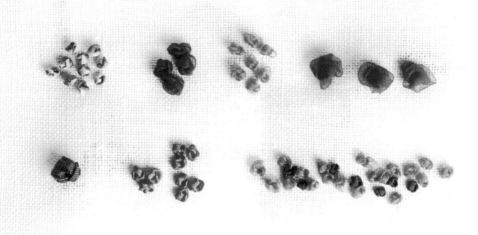

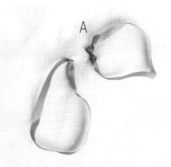

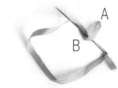

1. Bring the needle out at A and form a loop of ribbon flat against the fabric.

2. Insert the needle at B, inside the ribbon loop.

3. Slide the needle under the ribbon, then twist the ribbon twice around the needle.

4. Keeping a firm hold of both ribbon and needle, bring the point up and to the right. Reinsert the needle at A.

5. Stop the needle halfway through the fabric and press the knot firmly against the fabric.

6. Shape the knot around the end of the needle.

Seed stitch template page 58

Pattern

To create the single seed stitches below, follow the instructions for the first step of the double seed stitch on page 23.

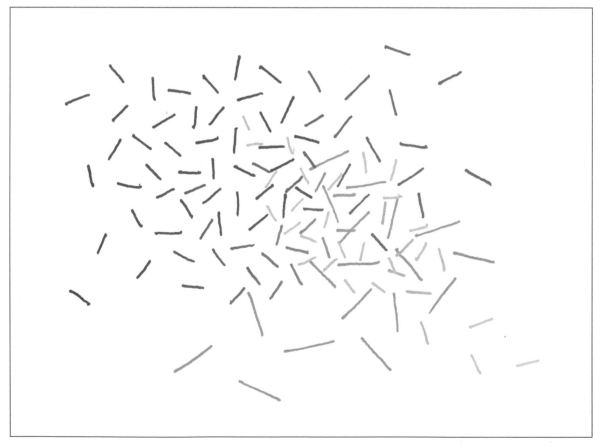

1. Bring the needle and ribbon out at some point in the fabric and reinsert it a short distance away to form a seed stitch.

2. Make another stitch of the same size beside it, not allowing the stitches to touch. This is a double seed stitch.

3. Make other groups of double seed stitches scattered over the fabric.

Tip Position the stitches at random—this is what gives the double seed stitch its charm.

Variation Change to another color of ribbon and make other groups of double seed stitches.

Variation Take another color ribbon and intersperse other groups of double seed stitches in the design.

Straight stitch template page 58

1. The straight stitch is one of the most basic embroidery stitches. Bring the needle out and reinsert it a short distance away to form a straight stitch.

2. You can vary the type of ribbon, the colors, and the length of the stitches to form interesting patterns.

3. Short straight stitches can be embroidered over the base of long stitches.

Variation Take a light, delicate ribbon and with just a few straight stitches you have a dragonfly.

Variation A sprinkling of short straight stitches embroidered over long straight stitches looks pretty.

Variation Using different tones of the same basic color produces some realistic shading.

1. Bring the needle out at A, insert a short distance away at B making a long straight stitch, and bring it out again at A (the center of the flower).

2. Insert the needle at C to form a petal the same length as the first and come out again at A.

3. Embroider three more straight stitches of the same length to create the five petals of the flower, all starting from the center at A.

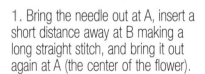

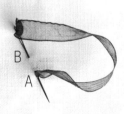

Variation Using a wide, sheer ribbon, bring the needle out at A, insert at B, and bring out again at A (the center of the flower).

Make another straight stitch of the same length to form a right angle with the first.

Repeat two times to create a total of four flower petals. Pull gently on the ribbon to give it volume.

Open loop stitch template page 58

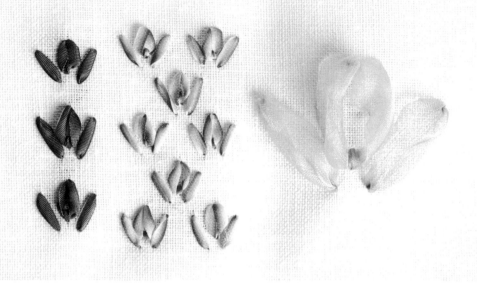

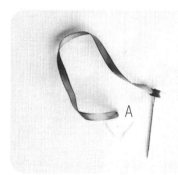

1. Bring the needle out at A.

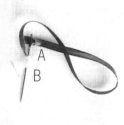

2. Insert the needle at the same point (A) and bring it out at B to form a loop.

3. Pass the needle through the loop and pull until the ribbon lies flat against the fabric.

4. Make a small running stitch over the top of the loop to hold it in place and bring the needle out at C.

5. Insert the needle at D and bring it out at E, to the right of the central point.

6. Insert the needle at F to make another straight stitch and finish the open loop stitch.

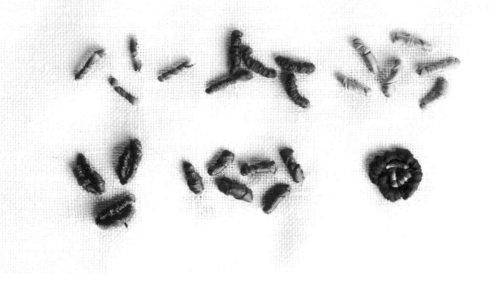

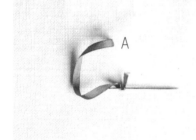

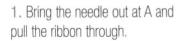

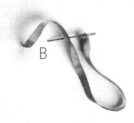

1. Bring the needle out at A and pull the ribbon through.

2. Insert the needle a little further along at B and bring it out again at A.

3. Twist the ribbon several times around the point of the needle, keeping a loop of ribbon.

4. Carefully slide the needle out of the spiral of ribbon.

5. Pull on the ribbon gently to close the loop and place the ribbon curl against the fabric.

6. Insert the needle at B and anchor the ribbon on the reverse side (page 12) to complete the bullion knot.

Small repeating stitches sampler

This sampler (illustrated on page 14) consists of four squares—one worked in seed stitch, one in Russian stitch, one in sheaf stitch, and one in lazy daisy stitch—bordered by lines in seed stitch, fly stitch, bullion knots, and French knots.

Size of pattern: 6 x 6" (14 x 14cm) • Size of fabric: 10 x 10" (24 x 24cm)
Materials: white linen embroidery fabric, 30 threads/inch (12 threads/cm); DMC chenille needles No. 22; assorted ribbons; DMC 6-strand embroidery floss; embroidery hoop

Pattern

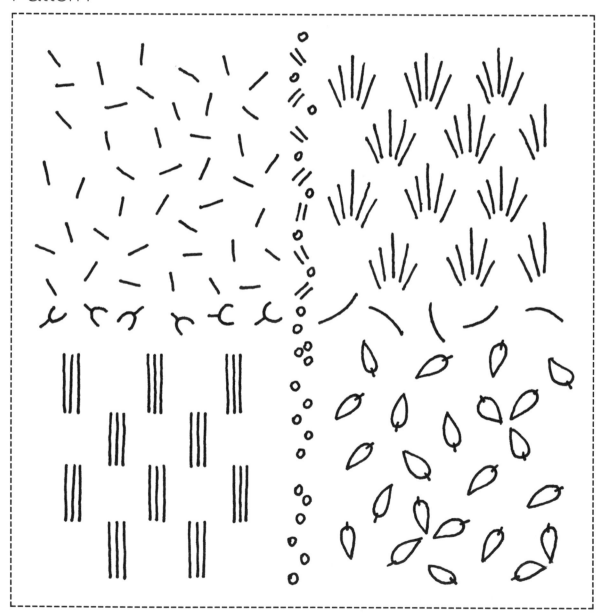

Instructions

- Find the center of the fabric and mark it with a pin. Baste along the lines separating the four squares with a line of running stitches to create guidelines.
- Stretch the fabric onto an embroidery hoop large enough to accommodate the entire work.
- Begin by embroidering the outline in backstitch using three strands of DMC embroidery floss, being careful to avoid the basting stitches.
- Embroider the dividing lines between the squares in seed stitch, fly stitch, bullion knots, and French knots.
- Embroider each of the squares in turn.
- When the sampler is completed, carefully remove the basting stitches.
- Press the borders of the fabric on the reverse side, avoiding the motifs; do not press the motifs as this would crush them.

Materials

Symbols	Stitches used	Ribbon	Colors	Width
4 squares				
	Seed stitch	silk	green	³⁄₁₆" (4mm)
		silk	violet with pink sheen	³⁄₁₆" (4mm)
	Russian stitch	silk	violet with green sheen	³⁄₁₆" (4mm)
		silk	green	³⁄₁₆" (4mm)
	Sheaf stitch	silk	green	³⁄₁₆" (4mm)
		silk	mauve	³⁄₁₆" (4mm)
		silk	violet with green sheen	³⁄₁₆" (4mm)
	Lazy daisy stitch	organza	mauve	⁵⁄₁₆" (8mm)
Dividing lines				
	Double seed stitch	silk	mauve	³⁄₁₆" (4mm)
	Bullion knots	silk	violet with pink sheen	³⁄₁₆" (4mm)
	French knots	silk	mauve	³⁄₁₆" (4mm)
		silk	green	³⁄₁₆" (4mm)
	Fly stitch	silk	violet	³⁄₁₆" (4mm)
Border				
- - - - - - - -	Back stitch (see page 38)	embroidery floss	mauve	3 strands

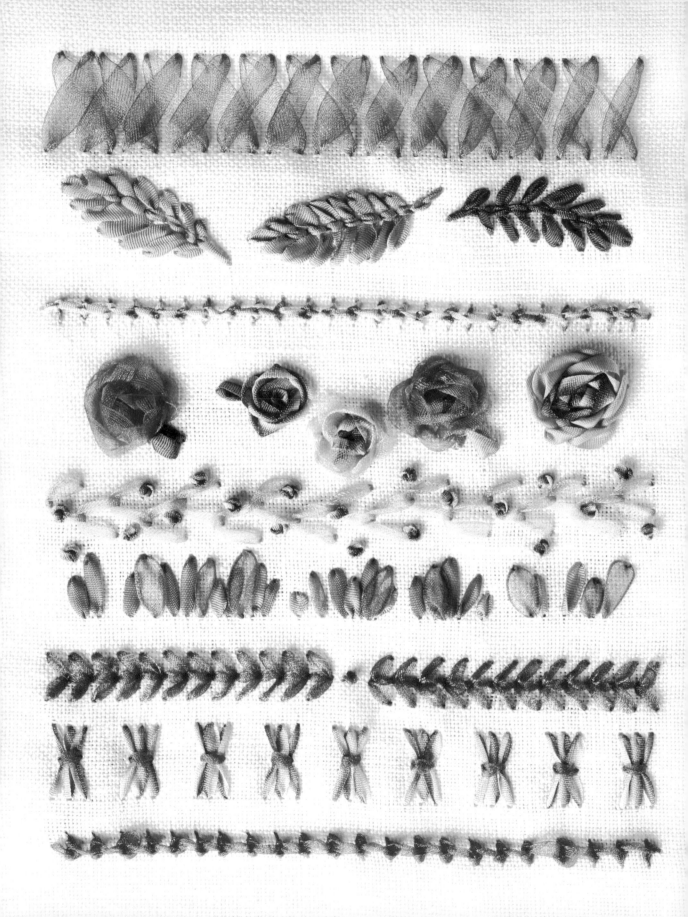

Line stitches

While they are generally used for marking out the fabric with straight lines, line stitches can be used as a decorative stitch as well. Try using them as a fanciful border—feel free to let them get sidetracked and wander off or curve. To make the sampler illustrated opposite, see the instructions on page 42.

Stem stitch

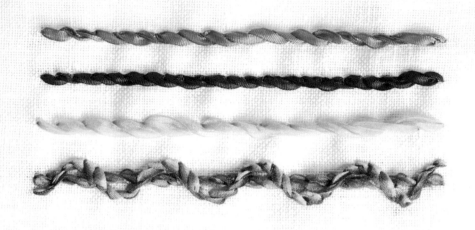

1. Bring the needle out at A, insert it at B, and bring out again at C, keeping the ribbon under the needle.

2. Pull the ribbon through and lay it flat. Insert the needle at D and bring out at B, over the ribbon.

3. Pull the ribbon through and lay it flat so that it overlaps the first stitch.

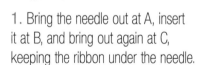

4. Reposition the ribbon below the line of stitching and insert the needle at E.

5. Bring the needle out at D to produce a continuous line of overlapping stitches.

6. Continue in the same way, always working from left to right.

1. Bring the needle out at A, insert at B on the same level, then bring the point out lower down at C.

2. Pull the ribbon through to form the first stitch, taking care to keep the ribbon flat.

3. Insert the needle to the right at D and bring it out again at E, passing it over the ribbon.

4. Pull the ribbon through to form the stitch, keeping it quite flat.

5. Insert the needle at F on the left side and bring out lower down at G, passing it over the ribbon.

6. Pull the ribbon through and continue embroidering, alternating the stitches to the left and right.

Split stitch template page 59

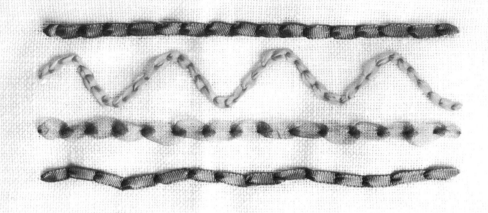

1. Bring the needle out at A and insert it a little to the left at B. Pull the ribbon to form a flat, horizontal stitch.

2. Bring the needle out a short distance to the right of the stitch at C.

3. Insert the needle into the ribbon near the start of the first stitch.

4. Pull the ribbon so that it stays flat and in line with the first stitch.

5. Bring the needle out a short distance to the right and insert in the ribbon forming the previous stitch.

6. Continue in this way, always inserting the needle into the previous stitch and keeping the ribbon flat.

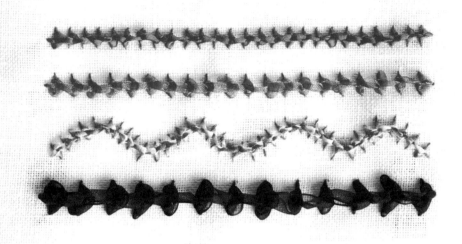

1. Using a single strand of DMC embroidery floss, make a long vertical straight stitch.

2. Make a series of straight stitches of the same length, parallel to each other and at regular intervals. Finish off the thread on the wrong side.

3. Using ribbon, bring the needle out to the left of the center of the stitches, take it over the first stitch, then slip the needle under it, point downward.

4. Pull the ribbon tight then slip the needle under the first straight stitch, bringing it out over the ribbon.

5. Pull the ribbon toward the left so that it forms a flat knot.

6. Continue forming similar knots on each of the straight stitches.

Chain stitch template page 59

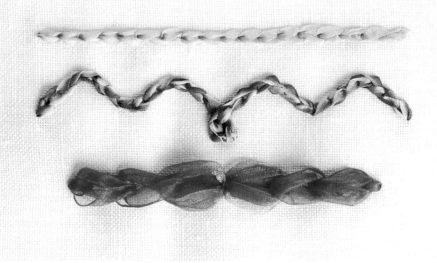

1. Bring the needle out to the front of the fabric then insert it back in the same place.

2. Pull the ribbon through to the back of the fabric, leaving a loop on the front.

3. Bring the needle up inside the loop and pull on the ribbon, keeping it flat.

4. Reinsert the needle in the same place and bring it out on the back, leaving a loop on the front.

5. Bring the needle up inside the loop, as in the previous stitch.

6. Repeat steps 3–5, making sure that with each stitch the ribbon lies flat.

1. Using four strands of DMC embroidery floss, backstitch (page 38) a horizontal line.

2. Backstitch a second line parallel to the first, beginning below the center of the first stitch. Finish off the thread on the reverse side.

3. Using ribbon, bring the needle out between the two lines of stitches at the left-hand side. Pass the needle under the first stitch of the top line.

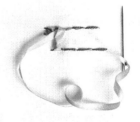

4. Pass the needle under the first backstitch of the lower line, pointing the needle toward the left.

5. Pull on the ribbon to form a loop, then slide the needle down through the second backstitch of the top line, and over the first stitch below.

6. Pull the ribbon to the left and continue in the same way, passing the needle through the remaining backstitches.

Backstitch template page 59

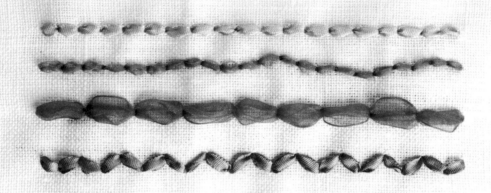

1. Bring the needle out at A and insert it a little to the right at B.

2. Pull the ribbon to form a horizontal stitch, keeping it flat.

3. Bring the needle out at C, making sure to align it with the first stitch.

4. Insert the needle at B and bring it out at D, then reinsert it at C. The stitches should touch.

5. Continue the line of backstitching in this way, taking care to keep the ribbon flat.

Note Embroidery in backstitch should form a continuous line with no spaces between the stitches.

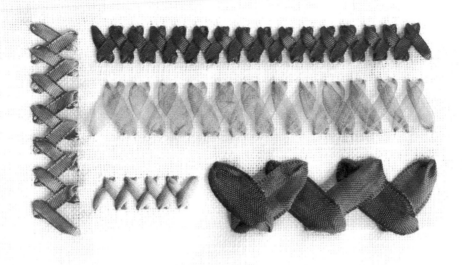

1. Bring the needle out at A on the front of the fabric, making sure the ribbon stays flat.

2. Insert the needle at B and bring it out at C to form an oblique long straight stitch.

3. Insert the needle at D and bring out at E, keeping the ribbon flat as it crosses the first stitch.

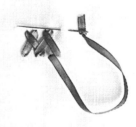

4. Pull the ribbon through, still keeping it flat, and insert the needle at F, bringing it out at G.

5. Pull on the ribbon so that it stays flat, then insert the needle at H and bring it out at I.

6. Continue the herringbone stitch in this manner, always making sure that the ribbon lies flat.

Double feather stitch template page 59

1. Lightly draw out the template on the fabric. Bring the needle out at A, insert it at B, and bring it out again at C, passing over the ribbon.

2. Pull the ribbon through and lay it flat. Insert the needle at D and bring it out at E, passing over the ribbon.

3. Repeat step 2, inserting the needle at F and bringing it out again at G.

4. Insert the needle below the last loop at H and bring it out at I, passing over the ribbon.

5. Pull on the ribbon, making sure it stays flat, then make another stitch the same as the previous one.

6. Continue the embroidery, alternating the series of loops to the left and to the right.

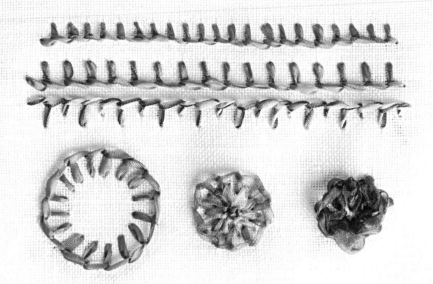

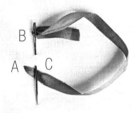

1. Bring the needle out at A, insert it at B, and bring it out at C, passing it over the ribbon, keeping it flat.

2. Pull the ribbon tight then insert the needle at D and bring it out at E, passing it over the ribbon.

3. Continue in this way to form a line, making sure the ribbon always stays flat.

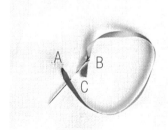

1. To form a circle, bring the needle out at A, insert it at B, and bring it out at C, passing over the ribbon.

2. Continue in a clockwise direction, inserting the needle at the center and bringing it out at the edge of the circle.

3. Complete the circle in this way, making sure the ribbon is flat when forming each stitch.

Line stitches sampler

This sampler (illustrated on page 30) is made up of parallel lines of stitches worked across a rectangle 5 x 7" (12 x 17cm). The lines of herringbone stitch, leaf stitch, raised chain stitch, woven wheels, feather stitch, straight stitch, fern stitch, sheaf stitch, and raised chain stitch are embroidered from top to bottom.

Size of pattern: 5 x 7" (12 x 17cm) • Size of fabric: 9 x 11" (22 x 27cm)
Materials: white linen embroidery fabric, 30 threads/inch (12 threads/cm); DMC chenille needles No. 22; assorted ribbons; DMC 6-strand embroidery floss; embroidery hoop

Pattern

Instructions

- Find the center of the fabric and mark it with a pin. Mark out the corners of the rectangle to be embroidered with pins. From the top to the bottom of the rectangle, mark the start and finish of the lines of embroidery with pins, checking with the chart for the correct placing. If you wish, baste along the lines as a guide for the embroidery.
- Stretch the fabric onto an embroidery hoop large enough to accommodate the entire work.
- Start embroidering at the top with a line of herringbone stitch and work through the pattern from top to bottom, finishing with a line of raised chain stitches. If you have sewn lines of basting stitches, be sure to avoid them when embroidering.
- When the sampler is finished, carefully remove any basting stitches.
- Press the borders of the fabric on the wrong side, avoiding the motifs; do not press the motifs as this would crush them.

Materials

Symbols	Stitches used	Ribbons	Colors	Width
	Herringbone stitch	organza	mauve	5/16" (8mm)
	Leaf stitch (see page 46)	silk	3 shades of green	3/16" (4mm)
	Raised chain stitch	base: embroidery floss + silk	yellow shaded yellow	2 strands 3/16" (4mm)
	Woven wheels	base: embroidery floss + silk	pink 4 shades of pink	2 strands 3/16" (4mm)
	Feather stitch	organza	almond green	5/16" (8mm)
	French knots	silk	shaded pink	3/16" (4mm)
	Straight stitch	silk + organza	3 shades of green green	3/16" (4mm) 1/4" (6mm)
	Fern stitch (see page 47)	organza	orange	5/16" (8mm)
	Sheaf stitch	silk + organza	shaded yellow blue	3/16" (4mm)
	Raised chain stitch	base: embroidery floss + organza	blue blue	2 strands 5/16" (8mm)

Filled stitches

Leaf stitch, fern stitch, fishbone stitch—the filled stitches with evocative names are like invitations to create something beautiful with ribbon. When these stitches are created, embroidery reaches its highest form and becomes a true art. To make the sampler illustrated opposite, see the instructions on page 54.

Leaf stitch template page 60

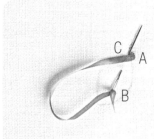

1. Draw a leaf on the fabric. Bring the needle out at A (at the tip of the leaf), insert it at B on the center line, and bring it out at C.

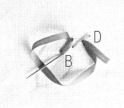

2. Pull the ribbon tight, insert the needle at D, and bring it out at B, passing the needle over the ribbon.

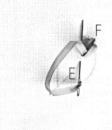

3. Pull the ribbon tight, insert the needle at E to pin the embroidery to the fabric, then bring out the needle at F.

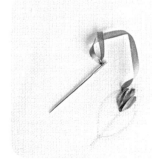

4. Pull gently on the ribbon, taking care to keep it flat.

5. Insert the needle at G and bring it out at E, passing it over the ribbon, which should be kept flat.

6. Continue to fill the leaf shape, adapting the length of the stitches to the contour.

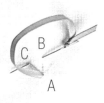

1. Bring the needle out at A, insert it at B, and bring the point out at C.

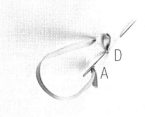

2. Pull the ribbon to form a big straight stitch (page 24), insert the needle at A, and bring it out at D.

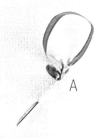

3. Insert the needle at A and pull on the ribbon to keep it flat against the fabric.

4. Bring out the needle at E, insert it at A, and bring it out again at F.

5. Pull the ribbon to correctly position it against the fabric then insert the needle at E and bring it out at G.

6. Continue in this way to form a series of straight stitches to create a motif of the desired length.

Satin stitch template page 60

Note Before you start, make sure the ribbon is long enough to complete the entire leaf.

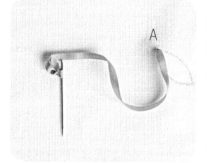

1. Draw a leaf on the fabric. Bring the needle out on the right side of the work at A (at the tip of the leaf).

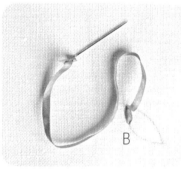

2. Make a big straight stitch, inserting the needle at an angle and bringing it out at B.

3. Insert the needle in the edge of the leaf, overlapping the first stitch slightly, and bring it out at C.

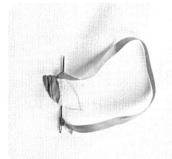

4. Pull on the ribbon to ensure it lies flat and make another stitch beside the previous one.

5. Continue to fill the leaf in the same way, keeping the ribbon flat and overlapping the stitches slightly.

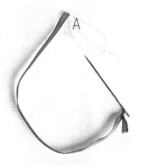

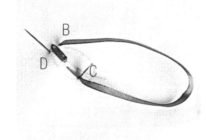

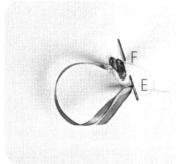

1. Draw a leaf on the fabric. Bring the needle out on the right side of the fabric at A (at the tip of the leaf).

2. Make a long straight stitch on the center rib of the leaf and bring out the needle at B. Then insert it at C and bring it out again at D.

3. Pull on the ribbon so that it overlaps the first stitch, insert the needle at E, and bring it out at F.

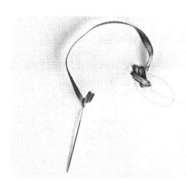

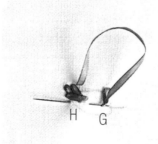

4. Pull out the needle completely and pull on the ribbon so that it lies quite flat.

5. Insert the needle at G and bring it out on the edge of the leaf at H.

6. Fill in the whole leaf in the same way, adapting the length of the stitches to the contour of the leaf.

Basic needle woven stitch template page 60

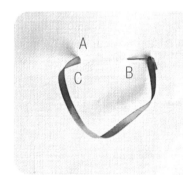

1. Bring the needle out at A, insert at B to form a horizontal stitch, and bring it out at C, just below A.

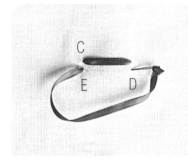

2. Pull the ribbon through, keeping it flat. Insert the needle at D, just below B, and bring out at E, just below C.

3. Make a series of lines of ribbon in the same way, parallel and close together. Finish off the ribbon on the reverse side of the fabric.

4. Using different colored ribbon, bring the needle out at F (at the top left of the parallel lines).

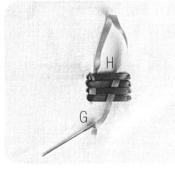

5. Slide the needle over and under alternating ribbon stitches. Insert the needle at G and bring it out at H.

6. Continue weaving the ribbon, alternating over and under at the start of each line.

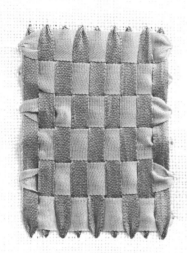

Couching stitch template page 60

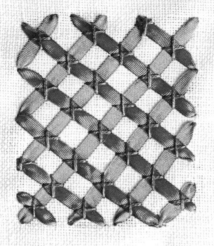
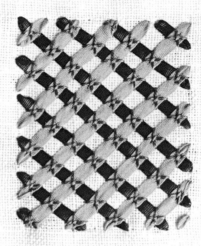

1. Make long, oblique straight stitches to form a rectangle, keeping them equidistant. Finish off the ribbon on the reverse side of the fabric.

2. With a different color ribbon, make long straight stitches in the opposite direction. Finish off the ribbon on the reverse side of the fabric.

3. The stitches will form a criss-cross pattern, with the starting and finishing points forming the edges of a rectangle.

4. Using two strands of DMC embroidery floss, make a small stitch at each point where the ribbons cross..

5. Form crosses by making a small stitch in the opposite direction over each of the stitches created in step 4.

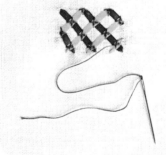

6. With one strand of embroidery floss in a contrasting color, make a small stitch at the center of each cross.

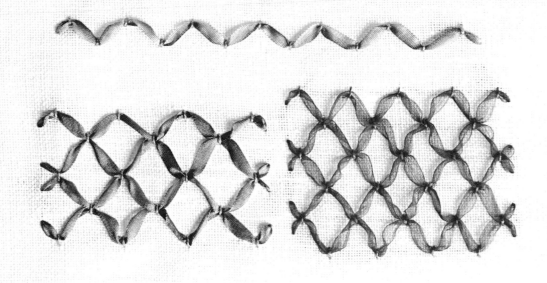

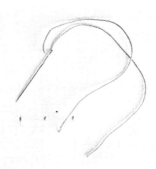

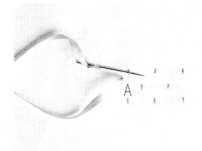

1. With a single strand of embroidery floss, make a line of small straight stitches and bring the needle out below, between the two first stitches.

2. Make a second line of stitches, spaced the same as the first, and a third line with the stitches placed directly under those of the first line.

3. Using ribbon, bring the needle out at A, to the left of the work, and pull the ribbon through.

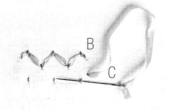

4. Keeping the ribbon flat, slip the needle through the first stitch of the top row and the first stitch of the center row from left to right.

5. Continue in the same way. At the end, insert the needle at B, bring it out at C, then slip it through the first stitch of the bottom row.

6. Continue sliding the ribbon alternately through the next stitch in the center row, then the next stitch in the bottom row.

Filled stitches sampler

This sampler (illustrated on page 44) consists of a 4 x 4" (10 x 10cm) square drawn inside a larger 6 x 6" (14 x 14cm) square, leaving a triangle at each corner. Each side of the small square is embroidered in a different line stitch—split stem stitch, oversewn stem stitch, raised chain stitch, and feather stitch—and each triangle is filled with a single stitch in a repeated pattern—lazy daisy stitch, double seed stitch, bullion knots, and French knots. The central square has five flowers and three woven wheels on a background of French knots in aniseed green embroidery floss.

Size of motif: 6 x 6" (14 x 14cm) • Size of fabric: 10 x 10" (24 x 24cm)
Materials: white linen embroidery fabric; 30 threads/inch (12 threads/cm); DMC chenille needles No. 22; assorted ribbons; DMC 6-strand embroidery floss; embroidery hoop

Pattern

Instructions

- Find the center of the fabric and mark it with a pin. Make a temporary guide by basting the outlines of the main motifs.
- Stretch the fabric onto an embroidery hoop large enough to accommodate the entire work.
- Begin by embroidering inside the triangles using lazy daisy stitch, double seed stitch, bullion knots, and French knots.
- When the triangles are finished, create the contours of the central square using oversewn stem stitch, split stem stitch, raised chain stitch, and feather stitch, being careful to avoid the basting stitches.
- Embroider the five flowers in the central square—two with violet centers worked in French knots and orange petals in lazy daisy stitch, three with fuchsia centers in French knots and orange-yellow petals in lazy daisy stitch, and three woven wheels using two shades of pink and pink DMC embroidery floss. Surround them with a background of scattered French knots in aniseed green DMC embroidery floss.
- When the sampler is finished, carefully remove any basting stitches.
- Press the borders of the fabric on the reverse side, avoiding the motifs; do not press the motifs as this would crush them.

Materials

Symbols	Stitches used	Ribbons	Colors	Widths
	Corners			
	Lazy daisy stitch	silk	shaded pink	³⁄₁₆" (4mm)
	Double seed stitch	silk	pink	³⁄₁₆" (4mm)
	Bullion knots	organza	orange	⁵⁄₁₆" (8mm)
	French knots	silk	orange-yellow	¼" (6mm)
	Lines			
	Stem stitch	base: embroidery floss + silk	green green	2 strands ³⁄₁₆" (4mm)
	Split stitch	silk	green	³⁄₁₆" (4mm)
	Raised chain stitch	base: embroidery floss + silk	green green	2 strands ³⁄₁₆" (4mm)
	Feather stitch	silk	green	³⁄₁₆" (4mm)
	Center			
	Lazy daisy stitch + French knots	organza silk	orange violet	⁵⁄₁₆" (8mm) ³⁄₁₆" (4mm)
	Lazy daisy stitch + French knots	silk organza	orange-yellow fushia pink	³⁄₁₆" (4mm) ⁵⁄₁₆" (8mm)
	Woven wheels	base: embroidery floss + silk	pink 2 shades of pink	2 strands ³⁄₁₆" (4mm)
	Background			
	French knots	repeated pattern of French knots in 3 strands of aniseed green floss		

Index of stitches

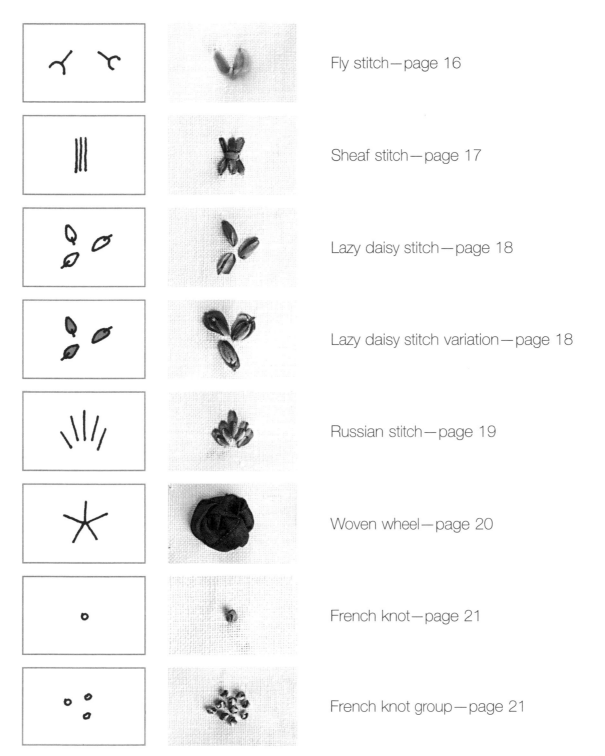

Fly stitch—page 16

Sheaf stitch—page 17

Lazy daisy stitch—page 18

Lazy daisy stitch variation—page 18

Russian stitch—page 19

Woven wheel—page 20

French knot—page 21

French knot group—page 21

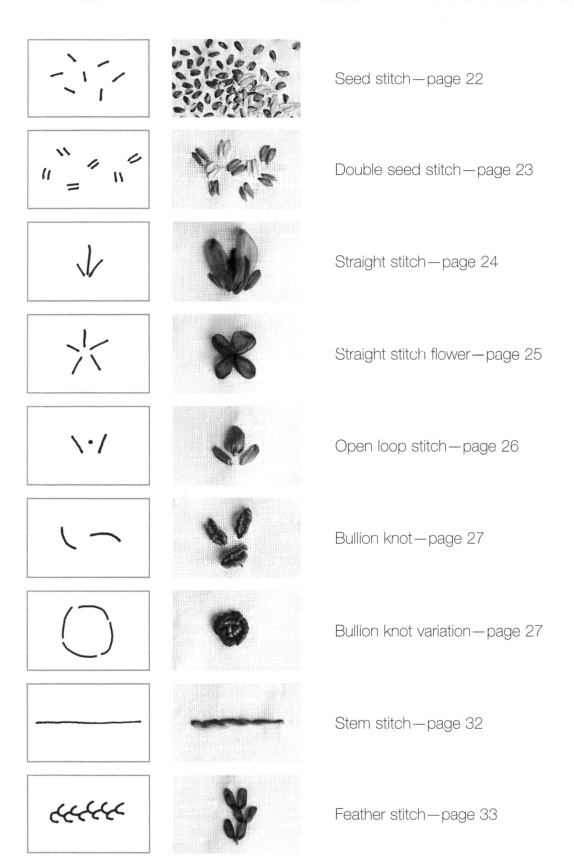

Seed stitch—page 22

Double seed stitch—page 23

Straight stitch—page 24

Straight stitch flower—page 25

Open loop stitch—page 26

Bullion knot—page 27

Bullion knot variation—page 27

Stem stitch—page 32

Feather stitch—page 33

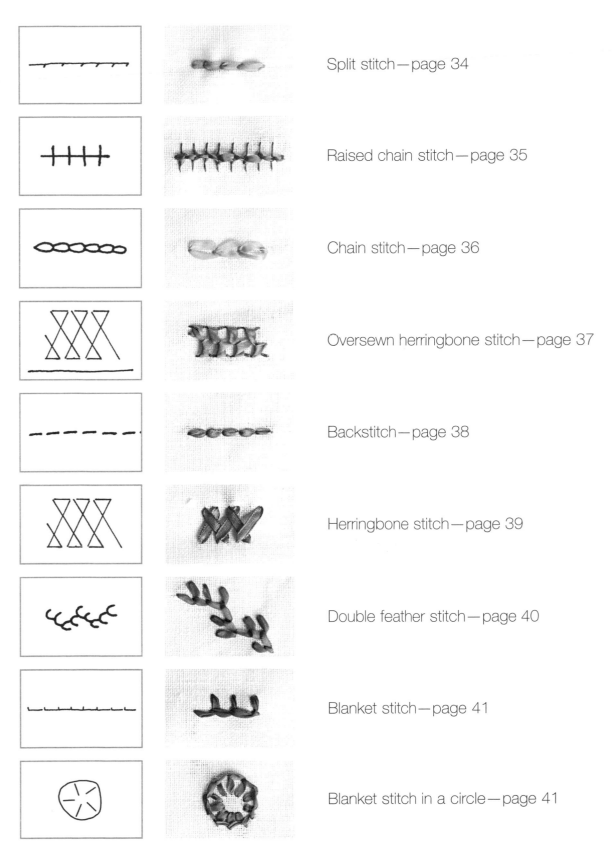

Split stitch—page 34

Raised chain stitch—page 35

Chain stitch—page 36

Oversewn herringbone stitch—page 37

Backstitch—page 38

Herringbone stitch—page 39

Double feather stitch—page 40

Blanket stitch—page 41

Blanket stitch in a circle—page 41

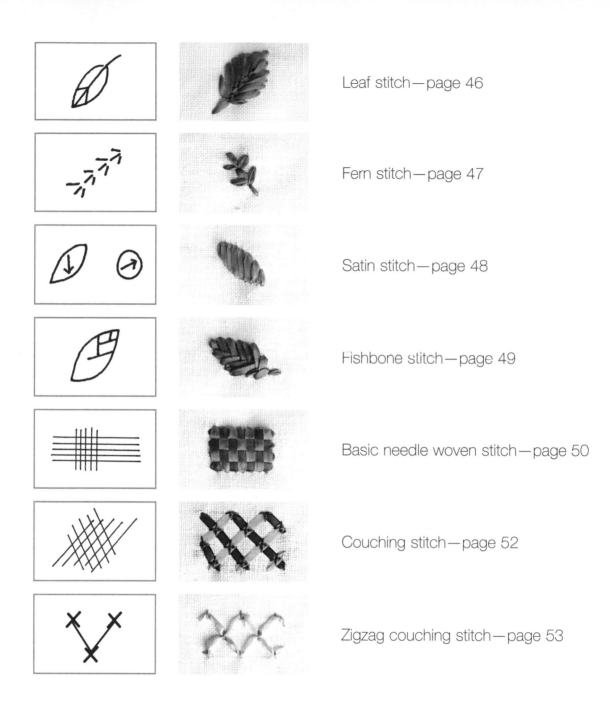

Leaf stitch—page 46

Fern stitch—page 47

Satin stitch—page 48

Fishbone stitch—page 49

Basic needle woven stitch—page 50

Couching stitch—page 52

Zigzag couching stitch—page 53

Index

Resources

Your local craft store or a chain craft store is the perfect one-stop shop for any of the projects in this book. Some specialty ribbon retailers are listed below as well—for when you need the perfect material.

General Craft Retailers

A.C. Moore
866-342-8802 www.acmoore.com

Dick Blick
800-828-4548 www.dickblick.com

Jo-Ann
888-739-4120 www.joann.com

Michaels
800-642-4235 www.michaels.com

Ribbon Retailers

M & J Trimmings
800-965-8746 www.mjtrim.com

The Ribbon Factory
866-827-6431 www.ribbonfactory.com

Ribbon Shop
877-742-5142 www.ribbonshop.com

The Ribbonerie Inc.
415-626-6184 www.theribbonerie.com

The Ribbonry
419-872-0073 www.ribbonry.com

Mood Fabrics
212-730-5003 www.moodfabrics.com

Tinsel Trading Company
212-730-1030 www.tinseltrading.com

Acknowledgments

We would like to offer our warm thanks to the Mokuba company for their wonderful ribbons which were used to make all the creations featured in this book; also DMC for their linen fabrics and needles.

Published in the United States by Potter Craft, an imprint of the Crown Publishing Group,
a division of Random House, Inc., New York.
www.crownpublishing.com
www.pottercraft.com

POTTER CRAFT and colophon is a registered trademark of Random House, Inc.

Originally published in France as *Broderie au Ruban* by Marabout (Hachette Livre), Paris, in 2007.
Copyright © 2007 by Marabout.

Library of Congress Cataloging-in-Publication Data is available upon request.

ISBN: 978-0-307-45381-5

Printed in China

10 9 8 7 6 5 4 3 2 1

First American Edition

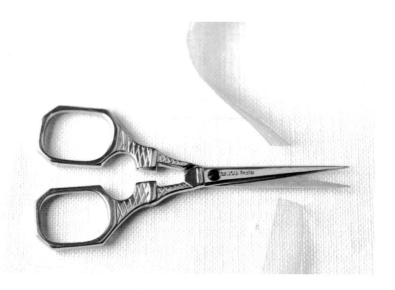